Balanced Assessment

Robin Fogarty

Training and Publishing Inc.

Balanced Assessment

Published by SkyLight Training and Publishing Inc.
2626 S. Clearbrook Dr., Arlington Heights, IL 60005-5310
800-348-4474, 847-290-6600
Fax 847-290-6609
info@iriskylight.com
http://www.iriskylight.com

Senior Vice President, Product Development: Robin Fogarty
Manager, Product Development: Ela Aktay
Editor: Amy Kinsman
Proofreader: Sue Schumer
Book Designer: Donna Ramirez
Cover Designer: Lisa Brutto
Production Supervisor: Bob Crump

Printed in the United States of America.
ISBN 1-57517-128-7

2354-8-98McN
Item no. 1684
06 05 04 03 02 01 00 99 98   15 14 13 12 11 10 9 8 7 6 5 4 3 2 1

Contents

Finding a Balance

How do teachers assess the totality of human potential, the development of the growth of the learner in all the interrelated realms? How do students reflectively acknowledge the changes and the development within themselves as they learn, grow, and progress? How do teachers authentically, yet practically, measure and assess?

Assessment is about measuring what one knows and can do and what one doesn't know and cannot do. Yet, if the true mission of teaching is to help students learn, the measurement must foster growth and development. It must not close the gates to opportunity but, rather, open the gateways of potential.

If this premise is accepted, assessment must be authentic, dynamic, fluid, and formative. That is not to say that normative, standardized evaluations have no place in the overall assessment scheme.

What is needed is a combination and balance of assessment practices. The tri-assessment model promotes using traditional assessments along with portfolio and performance assessments (see Figure 1). All three of these methods utilize Gardner's multiple intelligences theory and ensure both formative assessment of growth and development and normative evaluation of grades and rankings.

SkyLight Training and Publishing Inc.

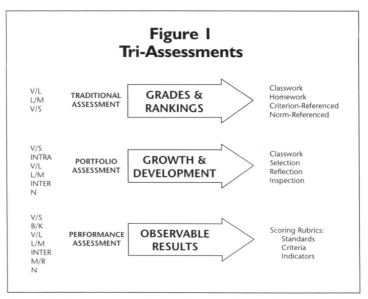

Figure I
Tri-Assessments

Adapted from *Integrating Curricula with Multiple Intelligences: Teams, Themes, and Threads*, by Robin Fogarty and Judy Stoehr. © 1995 by IRI/SkyLight Training and Publishing, Inc. Reprinted with permission of SkyLight Training and Publishing Inc., Arlington Heights, IL.

The Tri-Assessment Model

In the process of integrating content by developing significant themes and by threading life skills through subject matter, the lines begin to blur between disciplines. While some blurring of disciplines is desirable to create holistic, project-oriented learning, too much blurring causes concern about valid assessments, grades, and traditional discipline-based evaluations. In many cases, schools that use authentic learning and the multiple intelligences theory to move toward an integrated curriculum continue to use traditional assessment measures to determine grades, grade-point averages, and rankings. However, these measures don't always match active, holistic learning models.

The tri-assessment model provides a reasonable compromise for teachers who are moving toward more authentic assessments but are reluctant to totally abandon more traditional measures. By combining portfolio and performance assessments with traditional assessments, a truer, more holistic look at students is permitted. Each assessment targets a focus as well as specific features that are practical and relevant to the total picture. Each assessment also targets multiple intelligences to assess a wider range of human potential.

Gardner's Multiple Intelligences Theory

To tap into the full range of human potential, Gardner's eight intelligences seem not only appropriate, but, in fact, perfectly tailored as expressive tools for today's classrooms. Usually regarded as ways of knowing and learning, Gardner's intelligences are more than just receptive tools. Not only do students learn through the verbal, logical, visual, bodily, musical, interpersonal, intrapersonal, and naturalist channels, but teachers can easily use the eight intelligences as tools of assessment and evaluation. Figure 2 briefly defines each of the eight intelligences.

Traditional

Traditional assessment often focuses on grades, grade-point averages, and rankings. Included in traditional assessments are class work, homework, and criterion-referenced and standardized measures. In this situation, teachers teach and test students. Teachers retain control of assessment (see Figure 3). Typically, traditional assessments tap primarily the verbal/linguistic and the logical/mathematical intelligences, although the visual/spatial may also be included (see Figure 4).

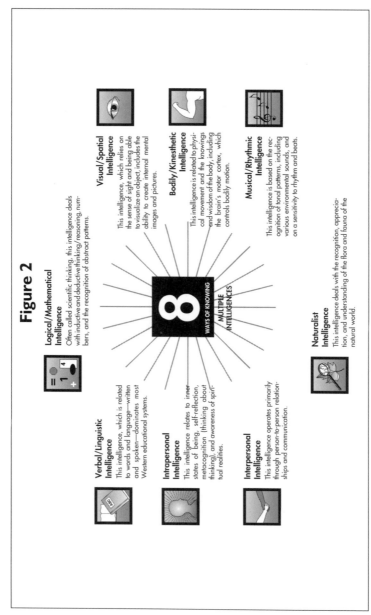

Figure 2

Logical/Mathematical Intelligence

Often called scientific thinking, this intelligence deals with inductive and deductive thinking/reasoning, numbers, and the recognition of abstract patterns.

Visual/Spatial Intelligence

This intelligence, which relies on the sense of sight and being able to visualize an object, includes the ability to create internal mental images and pictures.

Bodily/Kinesthetic Intelligence

This intelligence is related to physical movement and the knowings and wisdom of the body, including the brain's motor cortex, which controls bodily motion.

Musical/Rhythmic Intelligence

This intelligence is based on the recognition of tonal patterns, including various environmental sounds, and on a sensitivity to rhythm and beats.

Verbal/Linguistic Intelligence

This intelligence, which is related to words and language—written and spoken—dominates most Western educational systems.

Intrapersonal Intelligence

This intelligence relates to inner states of being, self-reflection, metacognition (thinking about thinking), and awareness of spiritual realities.

Interpersonal Intelligence

This intelligence operates primarily through person-to-person relationships and communication.

Naturalist Intelligence

This intelligence deals with the recognition, appreciation, and understanding of the flora and fauna of the natural world.

(center graphic: **8 WAYS OF KNOWING** / MULTIPLE INTELLIGENCES)

From *Eight Ways of Teaching: The Artistry of Teaching with Multiple Intelligences*, 3rd ed., by David Lazear. © 1999 by SkyLight Training and Publishing Inc. Reprinted with permission of SkyLight Training and Publishing Inc., Arlington Heights, IL.

Figure 3
Traditional Assessment
You Teach Me and Test Me

Figure 4
Traditional Assessment: A Checklist

Multiple Intelligence
Interpersonal
Verbal/Linguistic

Classwork?
❏ Participation? _____
❏ Quality? _____
❏ Frequency? _____
❏ Written assignments? _____

Verbal/Linguistic
Logical/Mathematical
Visual/Spatial

Homework?
❏ Is it done? On time? _____
❏ Is it correct? Accurate? _____
❏ Quality? _____

Verbal/Linguistic
Logical/Mathematical
Visual/Spatial

Criterion-Referenced Tests and Quizzes?
❏ Type? _____
❏ Weight? _____
❏ Accuracy? _____
❏ Completed? _____
❏ Quality? _____

Verbal/Linguistic
Logical/Mathematical
Visual/Spatial

Norm-Referenced Tests?
❏ Class rank _____
❏ School rank _____
❏ District rank _____
❏ State/national/international rank _____

SkyLight Training and Publishing Inc.

Portfolio

Portfolio assessment tends to focus on the growth and development of student potential. Phases of the portfolio development process include collecting and selecting items, reflecting on the significance of the items as indicators of growth, and inspecting the portfolio for signs of progress. In this situation, students take some control of assessment. Students get the opportunity to "show" teachers what they learned (see Figure 5). Often, portfolio development calls into play the intrapersonal and interpersonal intelligences as well as the verbal, logical, visual, and naturalist intelligences used in the traditional measures (see Figure 6).

Figure 5
Portfolio Assessment

Let Me Show You

Performance

Performance assessment focuses on the direct observance of a student's performance. Procedures for using performance assessment effectively include developing scoring rubrics and using predetermined standards, criteria, and indicators. Performance assessment also allows students to take some control of assessment. Students get to "do" what they learned (see Figure 7). With this assessment, the bodily intelligence becomes a vehicle for showing what a student knows and can do. The visual, verbal, logical, musical, interpersonal, and naturalist intelligences are also critical components (see Figure 8).

Figure 6
Portfolio Assessment: A Checklist

Multiple Intelligence

Collection:

Visual/Spatial
Logical/Mathematical
Verbal/Linguistic
Naturalist

- ❏ Over time? _____
- ❏ Number? _____
- ❏ Types? _____
- ❏ Quality? _____
- ❏ Other? _____

Selection:

Logical/Mathematical
Visual/Spatial
Naturalist

- ❏ Required pieces _____
- ❏ Self-selected _____
- ❏ Number _____
- ❏ Type _____
- ❏ Quality _____

Reflection:

Logical/Mathematical
Intrapersonal
Visual/Spatial
Verbal/Linguistic

- ❏ Rationale? (Why?) _____
- ❏ Context? (Fit?) _____
- ❏ Elaboration? _____
- ❏ Completed? _____
- ❏ Quality? _____

Inspection:

Interpersonal
Intrapersonal

- ❏ Long-term goals _____
- ❏ Short-term goals _____
- ❏ Overall _____

From *Best Practices for the Learner-Centered Classroom: A Collection of Articles,* by Robin Fogarty. © 1995 by IRI/SkyLight Training and Publishing, Inc. Reprinted with permission of SkyLight Training and Publishing Inc., Arlington Heights, IL.

Figure 7
Performance Assessment

Let Me Do It

From *Best Practices for the Learner-Centered Classroom: A Collection of Articles,* by Robin Fogarty. © 1995 by IRI/SkyLight Training and Publishing, Inc. Reprinted with permission of SkyLight Training and Publishing Inc., Arlington Heights, IL.

SkyLight Training and Publishing Inc.

Figure 8
Portfolio Assessment: A Checklist

Multiple Intelligence   **Standards:**
Bodily/Kinesthetic   ❑ Goals? _____
Visual/Spatial   ❑ Aims? _____
Verbal/Linguistic   ❑ Objectives? _____
Logical/Mathematical
Musical/Rhythmic   **Criteria:**
Interpersonal   ❑ Quality? (Completeness) _____
Naturalist   ❑ Quantity? (Time lines) _____

                             Indicators:
                             ❑ Range _____
                             ❑ High _____
                             ❑ Medium _____
                             ❑ Low _____

Adapted from *Best Practices for the Learner-Centered Classroom: A Collection of Articles*, by Robin Fogarty. © 1995 by IRI/SkyLight Training and Publishing, Inc. Reprinted with permission of SkyLight Training and Publishing Inc., Arlington Heights, IL.

A Word About Rubrics

Traditional measures as well as portfolio and performance assessments rely on preestablished standards and criteria; therefore, it follows that these criteria dictate how progress is shown. A scoring rubric is a typical tool used to evaluate fairly student growth. Rubrics identify criteria for creating a project and indicators to judge each student's performance. Figure 9 is a sample rubric used to evaluate students' knowledge about individual states in the United States. Using this model, teachers can easily construct other scoring rubrics to fit appropriate student contexts.

Figure 9
What a Wonderful State!

Performance / Criteria	0	1	2	3
Accuracy of the top ten facts/features listed about the state	Fewer than seven of the ten are complete and correct	Only seven of the ten are complete and correct	Only eight of the ten are complete and correct	Nine or all ten are complete and correct
Clarity of wording of the facts/features	Fewer than seven of the ten are clearly worded	Only seven of the ten are clearly worded	Only eight of the ten are clearly worded	Nine or all ten are clearly worded
Illustration of facts/features in the top ten list	Fewer than seven of the ten have colorful, accurate illustrations	Only seven of the ten have colorful, accurate illustrations	Only eight of the ten have colorful, accurate illustrations	Nine or all ten have colorful, accurate illustrations
Accuracy of city locations on state map	Good for one or two of the five largest cities	Good for three of the five largest cities	Good for four of the five largest cities	Good for five of the largest cities
State logo accompanying the top ten list	Not done	Identifies the shape of the state—nothing more	Identifies the state and at least one "top ten" fact or idea	Identifies the state and at least two "top ten" ideas

Adaped from Project Learning for the Multiple Intelligences Classroom, by Sally Berman. © 1997 by IRI/SkyLight Training and Publishing, Inc. Reprinted with permission of SkyLight Training and Publishing Inc., Arlington Heights, IL.

Multiple Intelligences as Assessment Tools

Using Ferrara and McTighe's "Framework for Assessment" (Costa et al., 1992, p. 340) and the multiple intelligences grid of activities and assessments (Burke et al., 1994, p. 36) to complete the Tri-Assessment Chart of Multiple Intelligences (see Figure 10), teachers have a ready reference to guide their assessment plans. By selecting a tool from each of the three major assessment categories, a trio of traditional, portfolio, and performance assessments are targeted to give balance and breadth to the evaluation process.

For example, a classroom unit on invention not only adapts easily to the tri-assessment system but also taps into a combination of intelligences. Students may sketch and label their inventions in a traditional task and, at the same time, build on the inventions as a semester-long project for the spring science fair. Pictures of the display become a viable part of a portfolio collection. To complete the trio of assessments, students demonstrate their inventions and are graded on their performance with a scoring rubric.

Most will prefer to use the Tri-Assessment Chart of Multiple Intelligences by selecting three tools for each intelligence, moving horizontally across the columns. However, a look at the vertical columns is useful to reveal the categorical assortment of tools (see Figures 11, 12, and 13).

Teachers who use the repertoire of assessment tools consistently target various combinations of multiple intelligences. By including different intelligences as a component of the tri-assessment model, teachers inspect the full range of human potential.

Figure 10
Tri-Assessment Chart
of Multiple Intelligences

Assessment Category / Multiple Intelligences	Traditional	Portfolio (product/process)	Performance
Verbal	label a diagram; script; oral questions; biography; novel; short story	written essay, story, poem; bibliography; diary, journal	interview; monologue; dialogue; presentation
Logical	true/false test; symposiums; multiple choice test; outline; notecards	computer printout; research report; Venn diagram; matrices; time line; artifact registry	debate; argument; presentation; rubric; computer program
Visual	fill in the blank; figural representation; symbol; show your work; diagram; matching	storyboard; scrapbook; props; comics; art exhibit; pictures; concept map; photographs	videotape; slides; film
Bodily	model building; outdoor education; field trip	science fair project; models; lab results	science lab demo; dance, dramatic performance; typing demo; athletic competition; sport; game
Musical	mnemonics; rote memory; song; rhyming poem; choral reading	written rap, jingle, song, cheer	musical; instrumental demo; voice demo; audiotape; cheer; rap; jingle
Interpersonal	teacher comments; peer editing; pen pal; invitation	dialogue journal; cooperative learning product	wraparound; think aloud; e-mail; telephone conversation; student-led conference; round robin
Intrapersonal	open-ended essay; visualization; self-discovery; inquiry	goals statement; homework; rough drafts; self-assessment	monologue; portfolio presentation; student-planned conference
Naturalist	identify plants; categorize rocks; label star charts	catch butterflies; collect shells; gather insects	planting; observe nests; field trips; photography

Adapted from *Best Practices for the Learner-Centered Classroom: A Collection of Articles*, by Robin Fogarty. © 1995 by IRI/SkyLight Training and Publishing, Inc. Reprinted with permission of SkyLight Training and Publishing Inc., Arlington Heights, IL.

SkyLight Training and Publishing Inc.

Figure 11
Traditional Tools
(pencil-and-paper tasks, tests)

Verbal	label a diagram; script; oral questions; biography; novel, short story
Logical	true/false test; symposiums; multiple choice test; outline; notecards
Visual	fill in the blank; figural representation; symbol; show your work; diagram; matching
Bodily	model building; outdoor education; field trip
Musical	mnemonics; rote memory; song; rhyming poem; choral reading
Interpersonal	teacher comments; peer editing; pen pal; invitation
Intrapersonal	open-ended essay; visualization; self-discovery; inquiry
Naturalist	identify plants; categorize rocks; label a star chart

Figure 12
Portfolio Tools
(visual artifacts, representational and real)

Verbal	written essay, story, poem; bibliography; diary, journal
Logical	computer printout; research report; Venn diagram; matrices; time line; artifact registry
Visual	storyboards; scrapbook; props; comics; art exhibit; pictures; concept map; photographs
Bodily	science fair project; models; lab results
Musical	written rap, jingle, song, cheer
Interpersonal	dialogue journal; cooperative learning product
Intrapersonal	goals statement; homework; rough drafts; self-assessment
Naturalist	catch butterflies; collect shells; gather insects

Figure 13
Performance Tools
(actions, demonstrations, presentations, performances)

Verbal	interview; monologue; dialogue; presentation
Logical	debate; argument; presentation; rubric; computer program
Visual	videotape; slides; film
Bodily	science lab demo; dance, dramatic performance; typing demo; athletic competition; sport; game
Musical	musical; intrumental demo; voice demo; audiotape; cheer; rap; jingle
Interpersonal	wraparound; think aloud; e-mail; telephone conversation; student-led conference; round robin
Intrapersonal	monologue; portfolio presentation; student-planned conference
Naturalist	planting; observe nests; field trips; photography

Adapted from *Best Practices for the Learner-Centered Classroom: A Collection of Articles,* by Robin Fogarty. © 1995 by IRI/SkyLight Training and Publishing, Inc. Reprinted with permission of SkyLight Training and Publishing Inc., Arlington Heights, IL.

The completed Tri-Assessment Chart of Multiple Intelligences is a handy reference, ready for immediate use. Yet, teachers may want to either add their own tools to the lists or create an entirely new chart, personally tailored to the tools they favor or to the tools that fit more appropriately with their curricular content. Types of Activities (see Figure 14) offers several tools to choose from.

By using the Tri-Assessment Chart of Multiple Intelligences for its intended purpose—as a repertoire of assessment tools—teachers are reminded that many of these assessments are activities, too. Thus, the chart acts as an instructional focus as well as an assessment guide. In fact, that is exactly what authentic assessment is—real, hands-on application and use of ideas. Through authentic use, teachers easily assess growth, development, and acquisition of knowledge as well as strengths and weaknesses in the eight intelligences.

SkyLight Training and Publishing Inc.

Figure 14: Types of Activities

Verbal
Symbols, Printouts, Debates, Poetry, Jokes, Speeches, Reading, Storytelling, Listening, Audiotapes, Essays, Reports, Crosswords, Fiction, Nonfiction, Newspapers, Magazines, Internet, Research, Books, Biographies, Bibliographies

Visual
Mosaics, Paintings, Drawings, Sketches, Illustrations, Cartoons, Sculptures, Models, Constructions, Maps, Storyboards, Videotapes, Photographs, Symbols, Visual aids, Posters, Murals, Doodles, Statues, Collages, Mobiles

Logical
Mazes, Puzzles, Outlines, Matrices, Sequences, Patterns, Logic, Analogies, Time lines, Equations, Formulas, Theorems, Calculations, Computations, Syllogisms, Codes, Games, Probabilities, Fractions

Musical
Performance, Songs, Musicals, Instruments, Rhythms, Compositions, Harmonies, Chords, Trios/Duos, Quartets, Beat, Melodies, Raps, Jingles, Choral readings, Scores, Acappella choirs

Interpersonal
Group projects, Group tasks, Observation charts, Social interactions, Dialogues, Conversations, Debates, Arguments, Consensus, Communication, Collages, Murals, Mosaics, Round robins, Sports, Games, Challenges

Intrapersonal
Journals, Meditations, Self-assessments, Intuiting, Logs, Records, Reflections, Quotations, "I Statements", Creative expression, Goals, Affirmations, Insight, Poetry, Interpretations

Bodily
Role-playing, Dramatizing, Skits, Body language, Facial expressions, Experiments, Dancing, Gestures, Pantomiming, Field trips, Lab work, Interviews, Sports, Games

Naturalist
Field trips (farm/zoo), Field studies, Bird watching, Observing nests, Planting, Photographing, Nature walks, Forecasting weather, Star gazing, Fishing, Exploring caves, Categorizing rocks, Ecology studies, Catching butterflies, Shell collecting, Identifying plants

Adapted from *Problem-Based Learning & Other Curriculum Models for the Multiple Intelligences Classroom*, by Robin Fogarty. © 1997 by IRI/SkyLight Training and Publishing, Inc. Reprinted with permission of SkyLight Training and Publishing Inc., Arlington Heights, IL.

References

Bellanca, J., C. Chapman, and B. Swartz. 1994. *Multiple assessments for multiple intelligences.* Palatine, IL: IRI/SkyLight Publishing.

Berman, S. 1997. *Project Learning for the multiple intelligences classroom.* Arlington Heights, IL: IRI/SkyLight Training and Publishing, Inc.

Burke, K. 1994. *The mindful school: How to assess authentic learning.* Palatine, IL: IRI/Skylight Publishing.

Burke, K., R. Fogarty, and S. Belgrad. 1994. *The mindful school: The portfolio connection.* Palatine, IL: IRI/Skylight Publishing.

Costa, A., J. Bellanca, and R. Fogarty, eds. 1992. *If the minds matter: A foreword to the future,* vol. 2. Palatine, IL: IRI/Skylight Publishing.

Doll, W. 1993. Curriculum possibilities in a "post-future." *Journal of Curriculum and Supervision* 8(4): 270–292.

Fogarty, R. 1995. *Best practices for the learner-centered classroom: A collection of articles.* Arlington Heights, IL: IRI/SkyLight Training and Publishing, Inc.

———. 1997. *Problem-based learning & other curriculum models for the multiple intelligences classroom.* Arlington Heights, IL: IRI/SkyLight Training and Publishing, Inc.

Fogarty, R., and J. Stoehr. 1995. *Integrating curricula with multiple intelligences: Teams, themes, and threads.* Arlington Heights, IL: IRI/SkyLight Training and Publishing, Inc.

Gardner, H. 1983. *Frames of mind: The theory of multiple intelligences.* New York: Basic Books.

————. 1993. *Multiple intelligences: The theory in practice.* New York: HarperCollins.

Lazear, D. 1998. *Eight ways of teaching: The artistry of teaching with multiple intelligences,* 3rd ed. Arlington Heights, IL: SkyLight Training and Publishing Inc.

Roth, Karen. 1998. *The naturalist intelligence: An introduction to Gardner's eighth intelligence.* Arlington Heights, IL: SkyLight Training and Publishing, Inc.

There are
one-story intellects,
two-story intellects, and three-story
intellects with skylights. All fact collectors, who
have no aim beyond their facts, are one-story men. Two-story men
compare, reason, generalize, using the labors of the fact collectors as
well as their own. Three-story men idealize, imagine,
predict—their best illumination comes from
above, through the skylight.
—*Oliver Wendell*
Holmes

Training and Publishing Inc.